Tip of the Quill

By
Muriel Jane

PublishAmerica
Baltimore

© 2007 by Muriel Jane.
All rights reserved. No part of this book may be reproduced, stored in a retrieval system or transmitted in any form or by any means without the prior written permission of the publishers, except by a reviewer who may quote brief passages in a review to be printed in a newspaper, magazine or journal.

First printing

All characters in this work are fictitious, and any resemblance to real persons, living or dead, is coincidental.

At the specific preference of the author, PublishAmerica allowed this work to remain exactly as the author intended, verbatim, without editorial input.

ISBN: 1-4241-9074-6
PUBLISHED BY PUBLISHAMERICA, LLLP
www.publishamerica.com
Baltimore

Printed in the United States of America

Dedication

To my children:

Samantha(1992–1996), Natalie(1994–1996),
Copelyn, Stenton, Justin and Alexis

Never give up on your dreams.
Anything is possible if you fight for what you believe in.
Believe in yourself and you will fly.

Love Always and Forever.
Mom.

Poetry Index

1. A Broken Heart 9
2. Honesty 10
3. Respect 11
4. Lies 12
5. You Dad 13
6. My Children 14
7. Dear Mom 15
8. Friendship in Chat 16
9. My Girls 17
10. To My Friend 18
11. Birthday Boy 19
12. Something Small 20
13. Colors of Life 21
14. My Daughter 22
15. Seasons 23
16. My Hopes 24
17. One with Nature 25
18. Remember When 26
19. My Dolphins 27
20. To China 28
21. Stars Galore 29
22. Grandma 30
23. Good-bye 31
24. Waiting 32
25. Darkness Within 33
26. Needing You 34
27. A Guiding Light 35
28. Goodnight Little Ones 36
29. Why Not Try 37
30. First Talent Show 38
31. I dropped the… 39
32. The Candle 40
33. The Water's Edge 41
34. Hanky-panky 42

35. For the Man I've Never Seen 43
36. Soft Touches 44
37. Time Is Ticking 45
38. Missing You 46
39. Thinking of You 47
40. The Toothache 48
41. Friends 49
42. The Song 50
43. The Playground 51
44. In the Park 52
45. Good Morning 53
46. Vegging Out 54
47. I'm Sick 55
48. Power of Music 56
49. Mother's Day 57
50. Just Another Day 58

1. A Broken Heart

I cry, and cry and cry
I'm left to wonder why
You won't share
Do you really care?

I've tried for many years
But all I got were tears.
I gave you my heart
But we grew apart.

You said you loved me
But I never could see
Did you even care?
Why never share?

I want to say good-bye
I just want to die.
Stop the hurt
Don't treat me like dirt.

My heart wanted to soar
But then you slammed the door
Why hold me back
I don't want to be in the sack

I need to move on
Stop trying to con
Be honest to me
Or I will flee

You, don't talk, you don't call
You make me feel so small.
Why do you hurt me so?
Do you really want to see me go?

2. Honesty

I loved you once, I loved you twice
unhappily we lived our lives like mice
One day at a time, the lies they flew
Right at me they came, made me sick until I was blue.

Honesty is all I asked of youI thought I had it, oh how untrue.

The truth stayed hidden, from me you kept
me in the dark as I slept.
When I awoke, the dark confined
I knew just then I only had time

Honesty is all I asked of you
I thought I had it, oh how untrue

Needing you to throw me a seed
instead you leave my heart to bleed.
My heart can't take it no more it won't
I beg you stop Just please don't

Honesty is all I asked of you
I thought I had it, oh how untrue

3. Respect

I beg of you stop the lies
The hurt for I can, not hide.
I bare my body, heart and soul
Life has surely taken its toll

Respect me I ask of you
Respect me I beg of you

The hours go bye
I can only sit and cry
I ask for respect
In return you direct

Respect me I ask of you
Respect me I beg of you

I'm losing the fight
Don't hold me so tight
Let me go so I can fly
Fly like a bird way up high

Respect me I ask of you
Respect me I beg of you

Soaring high and soaring low
No matter where I go
I will be free to fly
Up, up, up in the sky
Coming to my end
I wish some things would bend

Respect me I ask of you
Respect me I beg of you

4. Lies

Why do you tell me so many lies?
You must want me to just say good-bye
Everyday is the same as the last
Why can't I get passed, the past
Let me go, let me move on, I need to find where I belong
No matter where I go, I will always know
You will never be honest to me, why won't you be honest to me
If I could turn back the time, my head would with each chime
Fill with memories of all your lies
Years ago from our very beginning
We find each other terminating
No longer can I take your lies, they filed hatred in my eyes
Tears come streaming down my face
Just give me a little grace
Honesty truth no more lies, I want nothing but blue skies
You will never be honest to me, why won't you be honest to me
The lies you tell me, Hurt, don't you see?
I've tried to tell you, but you don't hear me
But I cry, and cry oh so blue
You care for no one only for you
You say you love me but yet you lie
Finish the knot with one last tie.

5. You Dad

You stand tall and wise,
You always heard my cries.
You held my hand when you were near
You helped me make things, when you were here.
You always taught me right from wrong
You said I sang a beautiful song.
You taught me morals, never to forget
You failed me with your regret
You spent Sunday afternoons with us
You would never, ever make a fuss.
You loved us all as much as you could
You did as you felt you should
You went to far, the cries they came
You did to me as the others the same
You didn't know I would be brave
You didn't realize my sister would save
You didn't think I would stand on my own
You were wrong I am, as I have shown
You never admitted to doing this
You hide behind something for all to miss
You need to be honest, wise and true
You taught me well, before you were through.

6. My Children

Children play every day
Outside, inside in every way.
Easy come and easy go
They go fast, and then they go slow
With their faces all a glow
There goes Alexis, watch out below
Down the slide, there she goes
Ten little fingers, and ten little toes
CJ, Stenton and Justin too
Brothers and sisters, through and through.
Sibling rivalry is never ending
Stop fighting, start the mending
All you have is each other
I can only be your mother
I'll live forever in your heart and mind
Please remember always be kind.
Remember the things I've taught you well
Live and learn and never sell
Honesty and truth will set you free
Live your life as you would with me.

7. Dear Mom

All those days, you seemed to be
A mother to us, we needed to see
A kiss, a hug oh how we cried
To feel the love from you we sighed
Our schoolwork was ours, for you did not care
We struggled to succeed, but failed to share
Feelings remain in silence, how are we to know
Words of emptiness, fills our hearts a big blow
We kept our silence for you would not hear
The words we've said that were so dear.
You hurt me so, I cry so much
A mother's love and her very touch
Is all I ever wanted to hold dear
But never will I, have it near.
I've given up on wishful thinking
A true mother, you sure are stinking
I hate you now more then ever
Our relationship, I'll always sever.

8. Friendship in Chat

Friendship is a beautiful thing,
Angels sent to us when in need
Big or small they come in all sizes
From near and far here and there
When you least expect it there they are
Big problems and little problems
Lets chat, coffee or drinks one would say
Lets get together soon one day
Far and wide we all live in one world
We share the same feelings, thoughts and dreams
Some of us honest most of them not
Why is it so hard to be honest with one?
We reach out to others offering our hands
Some accept gladly others rudely withdraw
Chartrooms are grand at times and sad at others
People from all over the world come together
To laugh and cry to play and to sigh
The friends we meet along the way.
We learn new things each and every day
A big information center at the tips of our fingers
Our friends are full of information use them well
Make your life full of love and friends.

9. My Girls

Blonde hair and blue eyes, Smiles from ear to ear
Never seeing you in tears, Laughing is what everyone hears
Late night French fries, our nightly walks
I cherish them always. I surely miss our talks.
Good and bad times, there were all kinds
The fun we had playing while you were here.
I miss you so much, a hug, a kiss, and a prayer
To hold you tight, each and every night
Your names and birth dates are written on a dish
In honour of you, to remind us of a wish
Angels you will stay forever and ever
I miss you so much, Forget you, we will never.

10. To My Friend

Witty and charming, Dazzling and Darling
Always there when needed the most
A hug, a kiss, or even a shoulder to hold
Long talks, late nights, games we have shared
Misunderstandings along the way.
Friendship we share from the very beginning
Honesty and trust is what we have
Forever and ever it shall always last.

11. Birthday Boy

Today my birthday boy, you turn 8 yrs old
Remembering back, fondly over the years
Wanting so much just to have and to hold
Keeping you happy, never ever having tears
Smiles and laughter, what joy, oh what fun
A soccer ball, basketball, baseball or more
All the games you love to play under the sun
Your childhood won't last forever; it's just like the shore
One more game please was all you ever ask
Time is ticking, but school needs you more.
You're growing so fast, keeping up to you is a big task
I love you so much my birthday boy, go on make a wish
For your childhood always to remain; not for a toy or even a fish

12. Something Small

A 6 ft tall man feels so small
Needing arms to wrap around tight
Acting like a ventriloquists doll
Just wanting to lift you to your height
Open your eyes, heart, mind and soul
I'm here for you now and forever
A friend to the end, to keep you out of the hole
The darkness confined from your endeavour.

13. Colors of Life

Black the color of darkness, loneliness and despair
Yellow the color of a smile, warm, happy thoughts
Red the color of lust; of want, need and flare
Pink the color of love. Fills our hearts with knots
Blue the color of sadness. Tears come streaming down.
Orange the color of flowers; Wonderful smells in a meadow
Purple the color of mystery. Like searching around town
Green the color of life. Sometimes I just want to bellow
Brown the color of chocolate. Life keeps getting sweeter
White the color of snow. Pure and light, dancing all aglow

14. My Daughter

Big blue eyes, cute little nose
All the way down to your toes
Little fingers seem to grow so slow
The days they flew, where did they go
You started off small but grew so tall
No matter what we did, we always had a ball
Adventures came, challenges we accepted
No one was ever rejected.
Into a woman, you are turning
There is so much more learning
You will see, for you will be
My daughter always, just like me.

15. Seasons

Winter's snow, cold and bright
Shivering with all of ones might
Chestnuts roasting on the fire
Listening and singing with the choir

Spring flowers, and all the showers
Light jackets, and visiting the towers
Green grass grows a light wind blows
Playground fun, to the swings there he goes

Summer splashes, lake delights
Paddling the canoe, Taking in the sights
Nighttime songs around the open fire
The northern lights for one to admire

Fall leaves drop on the ground
Off the tree's from all around
Cold wind's blow, snow starts to fall
Skiing, skating and that's not all

16. My Hopes

Looking up at the sky tonight
I wish and hope, with all my might
That all my wishes, and dreams come true
Wanting so much, through and through
Life, is not kind, it's cruel. Don't you see?
All I ever wanted, was just to be me
To be given a chance to spread my wings
Sharing my talents, and all that life brings
My heart wants to sing, along with the song
Just wanting to find, where I belong.
A star in the sky, twinkling so bright
Show me where, I can find the light.

17. One with Nature

Sticks and tree's, the wind in the breeze
Can we sit and watch the water please?
The water ripples, the birds fly so low
Sun starts setting, lets head home slow
Getting cooler now, minute by minute
A sea otter swims by, knowing no limit
Not a care in the world, what a sight to see
My camera is broken and not with me
A butterfly flitters and flaps
Almost as if it was drawing a map
A bumblebee buzzes, from flower to flower
What a great way, to spend an hour.

18. Remember When

Remember when we were free
Remember when there was a lot to see
Remember when school was fun
Remember when we played in the sun
Remember when we took those adventures
Remember when we read those chapters
Remember when the rain came down
Remember when we walked the town
Remember when we played those games
Remember when we had nicknames
Remember when the kids were small
Remember when I had to crawl
Remember when we watched movies
Remember when we threw the frisbees
Remember when we paddled the canoe.
Remember when I said I loved you.

19. My Dolphins

Graceful and darling, swift and calm
Sometimes watching, is like a sitcom
Dolphins you be, always so free
Jumping high in to the sky, for one to see
When someone is in trouble, your first on the scene
Trying to save, when in the marine.
A magical creature you are to me
Dreams of swimming with you, in my mind I can see
A beautiful song, you sing all night long
The melody makes me feel like I belong.

20. To China

In a child's eyes, the world is big
In the backyard, a hole they dig
Trying to reach the orange, China they're told
Way down in the ground, shovels they hold
Where Rocks and sticks are what they found
Not a sound, coming from the background.
Mom is coming, hide quick
Staying out of sight is the trick
"Where are you," Mom did yell.
Everyone kept quiet, no one did tell.

21. Stars Galore

Starlight star bright, wishing on my little star tonight
Guiding those with your radiant night-light
Way up high, into the sky; Dancing around the moon
Twinkling through the night, dawn will near soon.
To bed the stars will go, the sun will say hello.
Some days go slow, some days go turbo.
The clouds may come, the rain might pour
But one thing is for sure; there will always be stars galore.

22. Grandma

I have your name we are not the same
You lived your life alone, why did you blame
All those years are gone you hid like a con
Drinking in secret, always withdrawn
We never knew, no one spoke a word
From you I wanted to be heard
To learn what only you could have taught
Your musical gift could never be bought
I'm told was heavenly, Opera was the sound
In competitions you always did astound.
Unfortunately for us, we will always miss
From ever hearing you sing, saying goodbye without a kiss

23. Good-bye

Do you really understand, you say you do?
To me I only wanted you to be true
You couldn't be honest, the truth you kept hidden
Like the apple from the tree that was forbidden
At first you were good, caring and kind
Time has taken its toll you have become so blind
To what life had in store, for you on your path.
Catching up is hard from your aftermath
The decisions you make are yours make no mistake
I can't not be with you, without me, you must partake
For you see, our relationship cannot mend
Unfortunately I cannot even be a friend.

24. Waiting

Waiting, waiting, waiting.
Always seem to be waiting
For him or her, they all keep me waiting
Why do I keep waiting?
Give me a minute, or two
I'll be right back. Never coming back
I'm getting tired of waiting
No more I will break free
From waiting for you and for me

25. Darkness Within

Darkness within me, kept confined
Thoughts deep, within my mind
Alone night after night, no one in sight
Wanting so much to be shown the light
Out of the dark, I want to be
Let me go, let me be free
Blackness surrounds, please be kind
To me, I need to have peace of mind
Together with another, take my hand
Lead the way home; I'm beginning to demand
To be out of the darkness that keeps me tied down
Breaking the chains, from always being putdown

26. Needing You

The ocean so blue
I wish to see you
Miss you so much
Longing for your touch
One kiss, two kiss three kiss more
Seeing you walk through my door
To have and to hold
I know I can be bold
I've lost my way
Come make my day
Take, my hand, show me how
I wish I knew how to endow
Rise above the darkness below
Needing to see the rainbow

27. A Guiding Light

I am tired, very, very tired
Wishing to hear, you're hired
Dreaming of that wonderful job
Reaching the door, turning the knob
On a sunny summer Sunday afternoon
Feeling like being lifted up, by a big balloon
Being carried far away, way up high in the sky
Learning quickly to soar and to fly
Spread my wings, stretching out far
With all my might, reaching for that star
To show me the way, the guiding light
I'll follow it always, for it's always right.

28. Goodnight Little Ones

Off to bed, say good night
Kiss me once and tuck you in tight
Snuggled in, the blanket she tugs
Wanting and giving you so many hugs
Sing our song, the nighttime prayer
Mom we love the songs you share.
Back to bed, sweet dreams little ones
The morning will come, and bring out the sun

29. Why Not Try

You always wonder why
But never willing to try
I try to tell you, but you can't see
Many times over, its time to let it be
Why can't you try without me saying a word?
No matter what I say I will never be heard
You hear only what you want
But my memory can only taunt
Me from what we once shared
I used to think that you cared
Until one day, you didn't say
You only were lead astray
For this was the day, I couldn't say why
All I knew was to say good-bye.

30. First Talent Show

As I sat and watched you today
Singing your heart out, on this weekday
The song you sang, was beautifully sung
With all the other kids who you were among
A tear to my eye, it crept there slowly
Looking at you, your voice so warmly
Filling my heart, and a smile on my face
Seeing you there, with so much grace.

31. I dropped the….

I dropped the plate
Wipe clean the slate
I dropped the cup
Please walk the pup
I dropped the bowl
I can see your soul
I dropped the glass
Look at the green grass
I dropped the spoon
What a bright moon
I dropped the fork
Would you like some pork?
I dropped the knife
Come see the wildlife.

32. The Candle

A candle burning bright
The flame being the only light
Burns so high, trying to reach the sky
Dances around, like trying to fly
Moving flame, here and there
Light the way. A big flare
Wanting so much to get a handle
On the bright, flame of the candle.

33. The Water's Edge

We walked along the water's edge
Watching the birds fly above our heads
In the water the logs floated by
The tugboats running down the river
Splashing water, way up high
Laughing and talking, I loved every minute
Wishing and wanting for time to freeze
Sunshine and warmth, if you please.

34. Hanky-panky

Hanky-panky sat on a train
Hanky-panky wanted an airplane
Hanky-panky started to cry
Hanky-panky knew he couldn't fly
Hanky-panky threw a fit
Hanky-panky had to split
Hanky-panky grew so tall
Hanky-panky loved nightfall
Hanky-panky planted a tree
Hanky-panky was only 3.

35. For the Man I've Never Seen

For the man I've never seen
You're the one I'll never know
As long as you sit over there
The distance we'll always keep
You don't want this no more
To be closer, to have and to hold
Me in your arms and in your heart
Looking deep in my eyes
Never having to say our good-byes

36. Soft Touches

Soft smooth slight touches
Running over a silky body
Satiny feeling, through the fingers
Electricity running through the veins
Up the arm, down the chest
Into the leg, right into the toes
Back up the leg, stopping just so
Right up to the shoulders, into the arms
Little kisses to follow the touches
The body shakes, shivers and flinches

37. Time Is Ticking

Time is ticking slowly by
Wondering if you, will ever say hi
I see you every, now and again
Sitting down I try to write, with my pen
Words that should have, been said
Hoping that I have not mislead
Time flies by without a doubt
One day soon I will fade-out.

38. Missing You

River so blue
I'm missing you
Ocean so wide
I often cried
Sea so green
Never being mean
Stream trickling down
Sometimes acting like a clown
Thoughts of you running through my mind
Hoping one day our lives will be combined.

39. Thinking of You

Sitting beside you on my couch tonight
Talking of being at the campsite
Thinking of what times we could share
Going to many places, and visiting the fair.
Summertime is nearing us soon
Spending nights with you under the moon
We talk of the children and how they played
The shade then grew and the sun did fade
Time to go home, time is ticking
I only wish that we were drinking.

40. The Toothache

I have a toothache don't you see
It hurts so much I wish I wasn't me
The pain is so bad I want to cry
Put me out of my misery I just want to die
I know the pain it won't last very long
But while I'm in pain I can't sing your song
I really hate being in this pain, oh what can I do
I can't afford the dentist bill, and I'm out of shampoo

41. Friends

Friends we have come and go
Those who stay, always show
Ones who leave, have learned all they can
Sitting down over coffee, Hi he began
How are you, How have you been?
Tired mainly, wishing I was nineteen.
Drinking coffee, friendly chat
Laughing so hard, I almost spat
We should go, to the movies soon
Then take a stroll, under the moon.

42. The Song

I sang a song, a beautiful song
All day and all nightlong
The pussy willows, and flowers in the meadows
Singing of all my sorrows
Kids quietly playing, music fills the room
No one to disturb, with nothing to presume
The words come out of my head
As if out of a book, I read
My heart cries out loud, in the song that I sung
Like hearing the bells that have been rung.

43. The Playground

You went to the park, with your friend today
You went and played; we did it your way
The games I've told you, be careful when you play
You played today, but now you regret, so you say
Trying to jump and, reach the one bar
Thinking you could do it, trying to be a star
Jumping to far, missing it, and hitting the ground
Only being glad, you had a friend around
Losing your sight, and your breath
Thankful it wasn't to your death.
Tears come flooding down your face
As you awoken, your heart it did race
Coming home as fast as you can
Going to the park without an adult I now ban.

44. In the Park

It's so beautiful outside today
Lets go to the park; what do you say?
The sun is shining, not a cloud in the sky
We'll spend the day playing, watching birds fly, way up high
Sit on the swing I'll push you first
Pushing so high, you almost burst
Falling to the ground, I try not to laugh
But seeing you fly, reminds me of a giraffe
Up the stairs, and down the slide
Come on lets go for a ride
The sun is setting its time to go
Nighttime is coming it's starting to show.

45. Good Morning

Get out of bed, you sleepy head
Morning is here, Good Morning I said
Go get ready, brush your teeth and your hair
You have lots of time don't despair
School bells will ring, an hour or more
Sit and watch TV or even do your chore
Don't be late, watch the time
Wash your face I feel some slime.
It's 8:30, your running behind
You can see the clock; I know you're not blind.
Hurry now, walk real fast, and beat that last bell
I love you so much; have a great day I wish you well.

46. Vegging Out

Laying on my bed tonight
Thinking of you and all things bright
Vegging out, just laying real still
Waiting on supper, my tummy it will fill
Not wanting to do, anything special
The movie that's on, there is a great battle
Thoughts keep running through my mind
Remembering how, you were always so kind
Wondering what you are doing at this very minute
Wishing you were here, wanting you to be my thicket.

47. I'm Sick

My head hurts, my body aches
I really wish I didn't have the shakes
My temperature is rising, I feel so hot
My nose is running it's full of snot.
The cold chills are coming; I'm starting to get cold
I have a headache please do not scold
I want to sleep; I can't seem to get warm
Under my covers, I cannot perform
Just leave me be, I want to be alone
For me to hide, under a great, big stone.

48. Power of Music

Music is my higher power
Any way, any day, any hour
It lifts me up, so very high
Almost making me feel like I can fly
Makes me happy every day and night
Holding someone I love very tight
My heart wants to soar with the music
Dance, country or even done in Gaelic
There is no difference it's all the same
Lifting me to heights, the mountains un-tame.

49. Mother's Day

Just a few words to say
How much you mean to me
All the times that we did play
For teaching me how to see
All the adventures that we took
Going to the park or walking the path
Or even when we explored the brook.
You always helped me when I had trouble with my math
Talking to my teachers when I needed help
Teaching me to tie my shoes, or even helping me rhyme
Always come running when I did yelp
You are to me like hearing the bells chime
For the very first time.

50. Just Another Day

Every year is the same as the last
Days they are going very fast
Tears come streaming down my face
Wanting to go to my favourite place
Watching the dolphins swim and jump
Feeling my heart race and pump
Wishing to be apart of their world
Instead under my covers I'll stay curled
Away from everyone under the sun
Far, far away, I want to run
Where no one knows me, where I can be
On the ferry for me to see
The wild dolphin's swimming, living free
What a life that would be. Don't you agree?